Doc A Messenger

Sequel to Josie's Passage

Story and Photographs

By – J.G. Eastwood

Design, Layout & Illustrations by – BJ Nartker

Published in the United States of America

ISBN 979-8-89395-825-6 (SC)

JG Eastwood Author
222 West 6th Street
Suite 400, San Pedro, CA, 90731
jgeastwoodauthor.com

Order Information and Rights Permission:

Quantity sales. Special discounts might be available on quantity purchases by corporations, associations, and others. For details, contact the publisher at the address above.

For Book Rights Adaptation and other Rights Permission.
Call us at toll-free 1-888-945-8513 or send us an email at admin@stellarliterary.com.

~ This book is dedicated to the many who walk on two,

saving the scores, which journey on four. ~

Introduction

Study of the Holy Scriptures teaches us GOD cherishes all that, which HE created, including the animals. HE wants only the best for them. From within the Old Testament, it is made known that GOD had a plan from the very beginning of HIS creation; for each of the creatures HE fashioned.

There are 74 BIBLE verses that talk about caring for the animals. My best-loved are:

Proverbs 12:10~

Whoever is righteous cares for the needs and the life of his beast.

Psalm 15:10-11~

For every beast of the forest is MINE,

The cattle on a thousand hills.

I know every bird of the mountains,

And everything that moves in the field is MINE.

GOD'S kindness to give us the animals shows HIS great love for us. The animals bring HIS great comfort, blessing our companionship with devotion and love, one for the other.

Throughout the Holy Bible passages abound concerning brotherly love; remembering those that are in bonds, as bound with them; and them, which suffer adversity, as being ourselves also in the body.

"Forget not to show love unto strangers; for thereby some have entertained angels unawares."

The word "unawares" tells us that we will likely not know who or when the opportunity to "entertain angels" comes. Angels will also be unrecognizable. We do not know who GOD is sending our way, therefore be hospitable to everyone.

I believe that angels appear to us in the form of animals. HE tells us that I will send them without wings, so no one suspects they are angels.

And…

This is where a story begins; the sequel to "Josie's Passage."

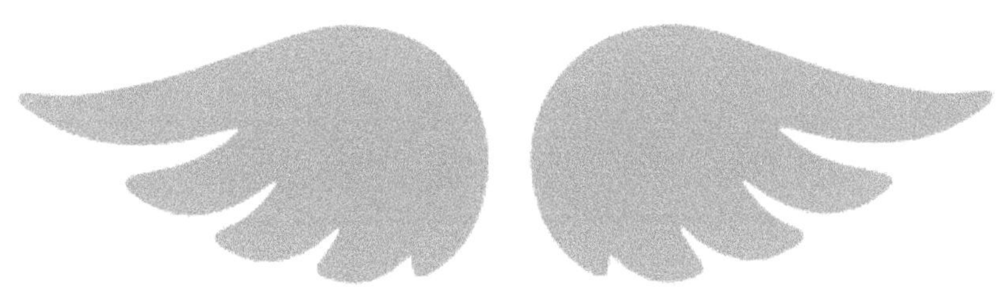

Preface

Before beginning the telling of this tale, I will reveal that I had no intention of penning a sequel to "Josie's Passage." If you have a copy of that book, or have read it, you know that Josie's medical records and information regarding her rescue are included in the volume.

I have no information regarding Doc. However, through deep empathetic observation, this amazing dog told me a story, and I knew that Josie's "passage" would pick up where it left off.

The story begins on a cold and rainy day, November 6, 2023, a very early Monday morning. Our immediate family, which includes two felines, two canines, and John and I, were not expecting a visitor, and especially at 7:00 a.m.

GOD loves the animals, and HE wants them to communicate with humans, demonstrating their devotion, love and loyalty by behavior and not words.

If you want to communicate with the animals, you can. Observe them, and encourage them to learn from you, and in turn they will give back this and more.

Now, at this point, I am turning the telling of this story over to Doc. I am penning this account as he communicated it to me, through body language and non-verbal cues; a silent dialogue, if you will, which as an empath, I, without question, understand.

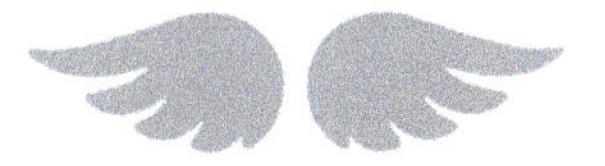

~A Messenger's Account~

What happened is beyond my understanding. Brought to this place by my owners, tossed out on a dirt back road, near a creek, cold, hungry and frightened, I asked, "Why?"

I had never been here. I sensed the feelings of abandonment and misplacement. I was cold, starving and shocked. I looked around, but I couldn't see anything that looked familiar. I was sad.

It was very dark, however, soon, a formless pale light was coming into view. It was not the sun, nor the moon, and it wasn't a star; just a single light. I continued to look at the light, and soon the illumination increased until it was larger and brighter. It blinked, and then it shot a beam, lighting the road, and then it began moving slowly. From where I had been put out at the lower level and on a creek, it traveled. A strange feeling came over me. It wanted me to follow it, and I did. The road was winding and uphill from where I had been put out at the lowest place, but I followed it.

I tailed the light for about a mile, and it led me to a leveled area, and once I caught up with the light, it flickered, faded, and then it was gone. But other lights were coming into my view. As I turned to see those lights, I saw a big farmhouse; the lights were glowing through the windows.

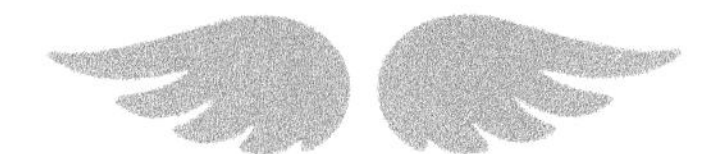

I ran to the house, and though there were lights inside, I didn't hear a sound. I spent the night on the large front porch. Though cold, hungry and frightened, I was happy to be sheltered from the pouring rain.

Sometimes during the night, I explored the yard. Early the next morning, I heard a back door open, and two other dogs were let out. They smelled me, and then saw me. The dogs were large and black.

The two teamed up to deal with me, chasing me around the house onto the porch. Their hackles raised, the two were barking viciously. I was terrified.

Suddenly, I heard a voice calling out to the dogs, "Y'all leave that skunk be!" Then a man appeared. He came around to the porch to see what the dogs were barking at, and then he saw me standing on the porch. I was not a skunk. He called "Josie" and "Wyatt" to come back into the house and they did.

The older man returned to the porch. He reached out his hand to me, and said, "Hey boy!" Then an older woman joined him, and they both greeted me. It was barely daylight; it was raining and cold. I was shivering and trembling, not just from the chill, I was overwhelmed with fear.

The man and the woman spoke to each other, and then the man touched me, patting my head. Trembling, I cowered, but his touch was gentle. He reached to pick me up, and I peed on the porch and myself, and I am not sure why I did that. With me in his arms, the man walked with the woman to the lowest level of the house, and into a room he called the basement. Once all of us were in the basement, except for the two black dogs, the man and the woman looked at my collar. They were checking to see if a name or number was present. They discovered that though I wore a collar, the metal bar tag had been removed, for the place where it should be was clean. The rest of the collar was dirty. It was orange and made of hard plastic.

The man removed the collar. Upon examination of my neck, he saw that the collar was too tight, and my neck was bloody and oozing. The lesion was deep.

The man told the woman, "I know he is a cattle dog, and most likely a Blue Healer."

Then they fed me kibble and I was so very hungry; I ate two bowlfuls. They gave me cool fresh water to drink, and they saw that I was also very thirsty.

The man carried me upstairs to the first floor. They took me into a laundry room, filled up a laundry tub with warm water, and then put me in. I was still very frightened. I didn't know what they were doing to me. But the water was warm, and I wasn't as cold. Then they soaped me, washing me from head to tail, and everything in between. They rinsed me, took me out of the tub, and then wrapped me in big warm towels, drying me thoroughly. Giving me a close going-over, they discovered that the tips of my pointed ears were hairless and tender. The woman asked the man, "What is wrong with his ears?" He answered, "Not sure."

The woman observed my behaviors the majority of the time we were together. She noted that I was scratching and chewing on myself all of the time. She kept a record of this. The couple then decided to take me to their veterinarian for a check-up and share with her that I had been dropped off on their farm with no tags, and ill-treated.

The day was drawing to a close, and to keep me safe, and out of possible conflicts with the other two dogs, I spent the night in the warm basement near a woodburning stove. The couple gave me more kibble, and a treat. They said, "Good night."

The next morning, the man saw that I had lost my manners, and he cleaned up the mess. He let me outdoors, and this is when he began teaching me to use the potty outside. He explained that Josie and Wyatt will show me.

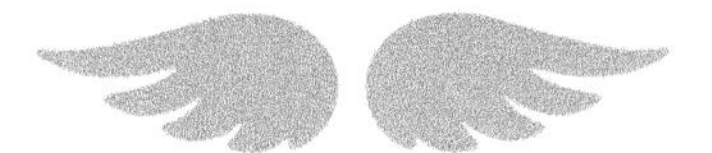

Then the woman came outside to join us, and while they were sitting in chairs, the woman was watching me. She saw me running, jumping, and smiling. She told the man, "I can hear him, John. He is telling us and himself that "I am free! I am free, and I can go anywhere I want to!" Then the woman shed tears; tears of joy for me, and my future happiness living with a family that would love me and take care of me.

The man gave the other dogs and me kibble.

Afterwards, the woman said to me, "Hopefully you will become a "furever" cherished member of our family, and your name will be "Doc." She continued, "We named the Labs "Josie" and "Wyatt" Earp Eastwood, in admiration of Wyatt and Josie Earp of the old west."

In keeping with the theme of Tombstone and the gunfight at the OK Corral, they named me "Doc," for Doc Holiday. It would take time for me to recognize my name when they called out to me.

That same morning the woman called the vet. Her name is Dr. Kay Geyer, and her clinic is named Cherrystone Veterinary Hospital, located in Chatham, Virginia. Since the clinic does not schedule appointments, the couple took me to see her that morning. We had to wait, and I was leashed. The woman saw that I had been accustomed to being restricted. She said to the man, "I think you will agree that this dog has been tied, and not allowed to run freely." He concurred.

There were so many cats and dogs waiting for their turns, along with their owners.

In a half-hour I was taken back to the area for examination and treatment. My people remained in the waiting area. Then the man and the woman were asked to come back to the examination room where I was. They sat down and waited for Dr. Geyer to join all of us to find out the results of my examination.

She returned to the treatment room and they greeted each other, and as I looked on, Dr. Geyer told the couple that I was a cattle dog, and a puppy around a year old. Then she told them that I had intestinal parasites; hookworms, and there was no microchip.

She informed my people that she was required to call in to Pittsylvania County Animal Control that I had been abandoned with no collar information or chip. She told the couple, "If you want to keep him, animal control will require a ten-day waiting period to ensure that no one would show up to claim ownership.

Then, the woman told Dr. Geyer about the severe scratching and chewing I was doing to myself, asking her if I had fleas or a skin condition. Dr. Geyer answered that I did not.

Dr. Geyer gave the woman a small plastic zip-lock package with two pills in it. She instructed that the medication was to rid my body of the hookworms. She told them she gave me a shot for rabies, and to give me Benadryl to calm down the scratching. She said, "I am happy that you are going to adopt him after the ten-day waiting period, for he will have a good home."

The woman said, "You were such a good boy! Let's take you home." She said "home," and I was comforted, and I was certain, somehow, that I would become a member of this family. Happiness was a good home and a family to love me.

No one called Animal Control to claim ownership of me, and after the ten-day period passed, I officially became a member of this family. My Mama and Daddy were so happy, they went to town and purchased a new soft collar and a name tag. On the tag was engraved DOC and my phone number. I was now officially an Eastwood! I had a phone number!

During the next four weeks, my family noted that I was silent, and they wondered why a dog wouldn't bark; not a woof, whimper, yap, or yowl. I was still adapting to my new environment and the couple, and the other two dogs. I remained silent, because I didn't have anything to say.

Also, during that period I stopped chewing and scratching myself and my ears and my neck healed. My Mama said to me, "You are doing so great, Doc, and I am so very proud of you. You will never be physically or emotionally abused again; I promise.

How did she know that I employed and depended upon this tactic to possibly prevent certain abuse from my former handlers. Yes, she and Daddy told me their names; Mama and Daddy.

I was happy and thankful for their care and love, and I told them this by jumping onto their laps, snuggling and licking their faces.

Throughout the coming weeks, I learned to alert Daddy when I needed to potty, and I went outside along with Josie and Wyatt. It took a while, and I would potty on the kitchen floor, because sometimes I just couldn't wait.

Josie, Wyatt and I ate our big meal at 11:00 a.m. Then we played outdoors until time to come in and take a midday nap. Mama and Daddy rested, as well, and then upon awakening, Daddy took us for a ride in the farm-pickup truck. Almost every day we took the household trash to the community waste theater, and sometimes Mama would join us, and we would just ride, and seeing the whitetails, turkeys and sometimes hawks, eagles soaring, and even a black bear was exciting, especially for Josie.

At first, I was afraid to get into the truck with Josie and Wyatt to ride with Daddy, so he would pick me up and put me in the truck, and off we would go. After about a week, I decided that I liked riding with the family, and now I am the first one to get onboard.

I experienced an afternoon delight, Daddy called, "treats." In the evening around 6:00 p.m. Josie, Wyatt and I would gather around a piece of furniture in the den called a "jelly safe." That is where Daddy kept the treats. With three treats in hand, he asked us to "sit." I didn't know what that meant, but I learned very quickly, that when I did what Josie and Wyatt did, I got that "treat." I now sit, when asked, but my butt doesn't work like the other dogs, for you see, instead of a long tail, I have a nub on my behind, and it doesn't work right. So, I sit on my nub. The treats vary, but my favorite is something Daddy calls "chicken strips." I love this time of togetherness, for once again, I had never been treated so well.

That year together, we celebrated Josie's birthday on November 17th, her fifth year, with cake and presents for all of us. I never experienced this before, and I liked it.

On Thanksgiving Day Mama prepared a turkey dinner, and she and Daddy shared some of the turkey with us, even the two cats.

Then it was Christmas, and "Santa Dog" left us toys and treats, which were wrapped up in Christmas paper, and again, I had never done this before. I knew I was loved. A special occasion came, and the other human members of the family that live far away visited us after Christmas, and Daddy and Mama introduced me to their daughters and their children. That was exciting, because I love my family, and the more family members to love me, the better.

The New Year, 2024 came and together we celebrated Wyatt's birthday on January 15th with cake and gifts. Wyatt turned five years old, too. I was beside myself with happiness and gratefulness, and I demonstrated this to everyone.

My Mama and Daddy said that I was a treasure and a "sweetheart," so we celebrated my birthday on February 14th, Valentine's Day.

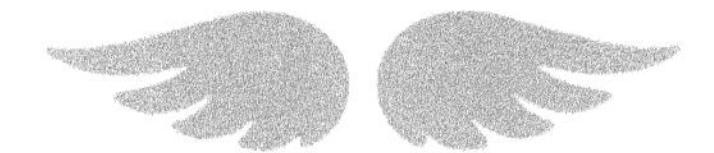

They didn't know the day or month I was born only that I had come into the world in 2023. I had a birthday!

As the days passed, I noticed the light from time to time, when I was out and about. At night it peaked at me through the windows or the kitchen door. I wondered if Josie or Wyatt saw the light. I realized that each time it visited me, I felt warm and comforted, for it was assuring me of my place here. I became close to Josie and Wyatt and loved them, and they loved me.

However sometimes, my behavior changed, and those actions got me into trouble with everyone. I started nipping at the legs of not only the dogs, but my owners, as well. I don't know why I was doing that. I just had to do it. Not too long after the nipping, I began yipping, and my first yip brought smiles to my folks' faces. Mama said, "You do know how to talk! What took you so long?"

When the cats visited the den, I chased them, I don't know why, because Josie and Wyatt did not. Then, my mouth got me into more trouble. I chewed on everything that I thought would be a good chew, especially plastic stuff. Sometimes I swallowed the piece of plastic, and it would get stuck in my throat. Then I would throw up, and again, Daddy would clean up the mess. He was very patient and kind to me. I thought he knows more about me than I do. My owners were patient with me, because they understood that these behaviors are characteristic of my breed, and that I was just a pup. Then I had the urge to herd Josie and Wyatt when we were outside, especially when we were headed for a ride in the farm-truck.

I was becoming a nuisance, so Daddy introduced me to something he called, "The Beep." It's a training collar with three modes; noise, vibration, and then shock.

When he needed to use it, because I wasn't paying attention to his commands, "No," "Not Yours," or "Stop," he advised that "I am going to beep you, if you don't listen." I learned quickly that, though the noise was not bothersome, the vibration was.

I am proud to share that my unacceptable behaviors are improving, and Daddy removed the collar. If I slip up, he reminds me of "The Beep," and I remember, and cooperate. Daddy never pushed the shock button, because he told Mama that he didn't want to harm me, unless I was in danger of running onto the road and getting hit by a passing vehicle. He never shocked me.

My human folks knew more about me than I did. Daddy grew up on a cattle farm, and understood my natural tendencies of herding and nipping, for I was bred to be a cattle dog. Through online search engines, Mama looked up, and learned about my breed.

She discovered that I am not a Blue Heeler. I am an Australian cattle dog, officially named a "Stumpy Tail." Now, I knew why I didn't have a long tail, because I wasn't supposed to have an appendage on my rear. And, to top it all off, my stump has a whisp of hairs, and because of that, they nick-named me "Stinger."

I have experienced a new life being a member of a real family.

It is Spring, and I am excited about the new adventures awaiting my participation. For the warmer weather will give us times together exploring the creeks, pond, and the farm. I hope I don't meet up with another critter Daddy calls a skunk, for I have been exposed to the "business end" of that animal, and it was most unpleasant. After the spray, Daddy gave me a special bath in solution of Dawn dish detergent, lemon juice and peroxide, which lessened the odor, but didn't rid me of the smell completely. Time has improved things, and I now smell like a dog should smell.

Four months have passed since I became a part of this family, and I have experienced so many wonderful things, which I didn't know about before I came here.

Life now is good, and I am excited about the days to come and the things I will experience, and the times we will spend together in discovery.

In closing, happiness comes when you least expect it. The journey led me to a new and wonderful life. I didn't know where the light was leading me, but I trusted it, and followed it to my destined purpose, and this will be talked about as I turn the telling of my story back to the writer.

AM I DREAMING?
FAMILY COMPLETE
WITH A BED,
BLANKET & BONE,
ALL MY OWN!

THEY TELL ME
I'M A STUMPY,
SO I CLAIM
THIS STUMP!

~ Follow-Up ~

In the beginning I shared that I had not entertained the thought of writing a sequel to "Josie's Passage." However, this little dog who appeared out of nowhere, on that cold rainy day showed us that he was special. John recognized that he was a herding cattle dog, but unfortunately, we knew nothing else about him, except that he had been mistreated and neglected. The indications of this were apparent; the severe lesion on his neck, bleeding and oozing, his hairless ears, which were tender, and his trembling, being afraid of us, and apparent hunger for food. He couldn't be filled during the first month he was with us.

After he trusted our care, and he was accepted by Josie and Wyatt, a story was born.

As an empath, understanding animals comes naturally. It is a GOD- GIVEN GIFT, which I have learned to embrace during my life.

Doc is a messenger; an angel if you will, and this little dog was sent to help Josie as she continues in her life's journey. The two dogs have developed a bond that has grown stronger with each passing week.

The photos included in this book are to share with you special moments that we were fortunate to capture.

After Doc joined our immediate family, we witnessed a gradual transformation in our Josie. Josie is very possessive of her toys, especially her green glo-in-the-dark ball. It serves as a kind of pacifier. Wherever she goes, the ball is with her. When we watched her sharing it with Doc, we were surprised, for she is not privy to give it up easily.

While John is playing with Wyatt and Doc, throwing frisbees and toy tires, Josie will lay it in my lap after mouthing it for a bit, and then she waits for me to throw it, so she can do what a Lab does, retrieve. She takes it to bed with her, and sleeps with it. She allows him to eat her bowl of food, but not Wyatt.

Once Josie and Wyatt became adults, they stopped playing together. However, with Doc, it's a different story. Wyatt plays with Doc outdoors and Josie plays with him indoors.

The inspiration for "the light," came during moments I spent with Josie. Josie's heart was filled with light, strengthening her resolve to survive. The journey of the light leading our Josie to many places and people, who helped her, finally came to a close when John and I adopted her. The story of Josie is extraordinary. The rescue group shared that her story was unlike any other dog rescue they had encountered.

Through the years, though she is loving and protective of both John and me, Josie grew closer to her Daddy, and he calls her "my girl."

After a short time, I saw in Doc's eyes that same light, and I was inspired to pen this book. He looks at us bright-eyed, overflowing with love and thankfulness for the new life we have given him. It was then. . .

"I saw the light!"

~History of the Australian Stumpy Tail Cattle Dog~

Though we knew that Doc was a herding dog, we didn't distinguish the breed, thus we didn't know the background of this canine. Upon legal adoption, I began my research, and I found that we knew a great deal about the cattle dog, however I discovered some amazing facts about this breed, which sets them apart from other classes of cattle herding dogs.

Per the search engines, photographs of the various herding dogs led me to one that looked like our Doc. Recognizing that Doc was indeed a herding dog, he was not a "Blue Heeler," he is a "Stumpy Tail." His tail was not cropped after birth; Doc was born with a stumpy rear appendage.

The "Stumpy" is thought to be Australia's oldest dog breed, beginning in the late nineteenth century. The breed's origin is not confirmed; however, it is believed that British colonists crossbred their herding dog with the wild "Dingo." Also, the class was initially bred crossing a "Hall's Heeler" and a "Timmon's Biter." The breed became very popular, for their work ethic, dedication to work, and high level of energy. During the 1960s, the breed became extinct, however breeders were successful in reviving the first Australian dog. In 1963 this dog was recognized as a breed of its own right.

In 1988, the ANKC formed to preserve the breed, The FCI in 2010, and the UKC recognized the breed as the "Stumpy Tail Cattle Dog."

The AKC recognizes characteristics of the "Stumpy," categorizing in classes of color and markings: Blue, Red, Blue Mottled, Blue Speckled, Red Speckled, and Red Mottled; markings in two classes, Black Markings and Red Markings.

Australia

Anatomy of a Stumpy

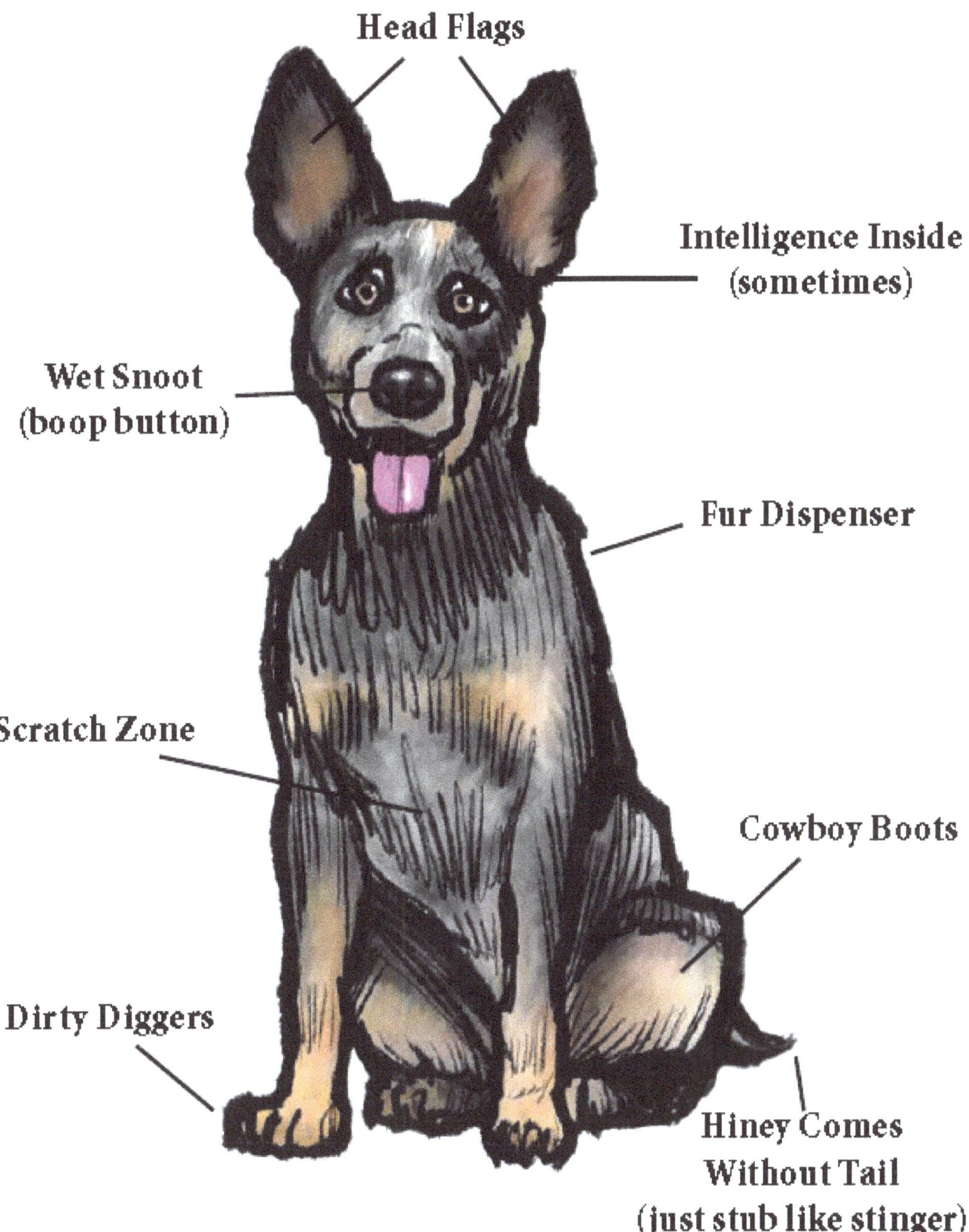

National Purebred Dog Day

Oct 15, 2015 at 1:00pm · 🌐

It has been one of the most shared photographs in NPDD history, and for good reason. Jeff Jaquish's photo shows the tenacity (and courage) of the Australian Cattle Dog. We feel compelled to allay any concerns for the cow who could easily shake off the dog at will. This dog, however, has established who is boss in this situation, and it ain't the cow. You can see it in the dog's eyes!

Our Doc is a Blue Mottled Stumpy, as you will note in the photographs.

~ Characteristics and Traits of the Stumpy Tail from the Land Down Under~

Average height of this breed is 18-20 inches for males, and 17-19 inches for females. The weight averages 38-45 lbs. for males, 32-35 lbs. for females. Our Doc weighs in at 40 lbs.

Average life expectancy is 12-15 years.

The breed easily adapts; however, it likes routine. They are playful and protective of their owners. The "Stumpy" is self-willed and their energy level is off-the-charts. They need to perform jobs and require out-of-doors activities. They bark to alert and are eager to please. Depending on the individual dog, some can seem aloof with everyone but their owners, while others treat everyone they meet like their best friend. Our Doc fits in well with the latter. Even after puppyhood, these dogs continue to play, and are enthusiastic to learn new ways to play. They get along well with other dogs and older children, however, because the inherited behaviors to herd and nip can be bothersome regarding younger children.

Due to requiring mental motivation, the breed needs to be happy and healthy. They require skills in decision-making, problem-solving, and concentration; without these, the breed will resort to self-inspired projects to keep their brains stimulated, and if they do not have this, they will find projects of their own, and more than likely it will be ventures you would not approve.

The "Stumpy" will usually want to make their owner proud, as is the case with Doc. He is enthusiastic to please us, and it excites him when he is praised hearing the phrase, "Good boy! Good job!" At every meal and with each treat, he thanks us. We feel thankful when he hugs and licks us. The expression in his eyes is nearly human-like.

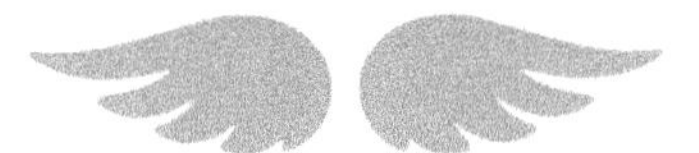

The energy level of this dog is to go at it nonstop. It is not optional, for the "Stumpy" thrives on the get-up-and-go mode. Doc loves to jump, run, chase, herd, and accompany his family, including the Labs, on long walks on the farm.

Doc is energetic, intelligent, alert, and occasionally territorial, however this is true of our Labs. As with the Labs, he is easy to train, not only hands on, but by observing the Labs.

Although Doc is a medium-size dog, he is strong, agile, and fast. John clocked him keeping up with the four-wheeler at 26 mph.

Though we no longer have cattle, we make sure that he is active when outdoors. During the evening hours, John trained him to settle in for the night. He has his own bed and blanket, though he likes to sleep near the Labs or John 's recliner.

I have read that a "Stumpy" is a good choice for anyone who can provide all of their needs. The ideal would be living and working on a farm with wide-open areas to chase, jump, run and just being the breed, he was born to be, a "Stumpy."

Doc is an Aussie Stumpy that is a spirit filled little dog with boundless energy, courage, doggedness, love, loyalty, strength, and I am proud to be lucky enough to share in his extraordinary life.

Doc is a Dingo. Doc is a devil dog. Doc is a sneaky thief, for he climbs the back stairway to a room where I feed my cats to steel the food. Doc has a "stinger." Doc is most gassy, and each episode during the passing is what we term an SBD; silent, but deadly. Doc is psychologically challenged, a forty- pound dictator with the supernatural ability to know how far he can push us to absolute senselessness before returning to a delightfully lovable creature.

Some of his tyrannical behaviors include, but are not limited to: stubbornness, dominance, territorial, excessively energetic, over-the-top nipping of feet and legs, jumping on us unexpectedly, knocking us off balance, frequently chewing anything and everything he deems chewable, and snatching Josie and Wyatt's toys, when he knows that they are not his. Finally, he attempts to seize Wyatt's long-established position in the farm pick-up, knowing that riding on Daddy's back, looking out the driver's window is Wyatt's spot.

Doc also moves things, pulling the particular item, such as the beds and blankets, and puts them where he thinks they need to be. He tuckers out afterwards and has to take a break. If you are looking for someone or "some dog" to help you rearrange your den or living room, he is your man!

But his endearing behaviors outweigh the naughty stuff, and we forgive and forget. We use consistent, firm and gentle training techniques to discipline him. He is rewarded with verbal praise and hugs.

Doc exhibits a behavior that we have never seen in any of our previous pets. Not only seen in his eyes, but with hugs and licks, he thanks us for meals, treats, praise, and kindness. We recognize easily that he is truly appreciative.

Since he has been ours, he has gradually evolved from being abused, and then abandoned, and fearful, to confident and content, for we have given him the greatest of gifts; love, security, and a sense of acceptance of his breed, and belonging to a real family. Doc is still a dingo. Doc is still sneaky. Doc is still a gassy dog.

~Australia's Outback~

The Outback is a very large region covering 70% of Australia's continent. There are 10 deserts and a sub-tropical area. It has the largest lowland, and the largest temperate woodland on the Earth.

The name "Outback" was chosen to replicate the idea of an outback, which is remote with a thinly populated interior.

The continent has three times more sheep than people. The predominant breed of sheep is the Merino, first brought into Australia in 1797. Other breeds include British Long Wool, and the British Short Wool, Lincoln, English Leicester, Border Leicester, Chevlot, and the Romney Marsh.

The cattle herd is 28.6 million head. The dairy breed is the Holstein Friesian accounting for 75% of the dairy population. Others include the Jersey, Holstein, Jersey, Brown Swiss, Ayrshire, Australian Red, Illawarra, Southdown, Dorset Horn, the Poll Dorset Suffolk, Texel. Additionally, the Australian Breeds, the Corriedale, Coopworth, Polwarth, and the Finn.

Due to the vast and rough terrain, the ranchers needed a breed of dog that could, not only manage the rough territory, but out class all other herding breeds. The "Stumpy" excels in trainability due to their superior intelligence. Their agility, energy, stamina, and their want to please their owners are off- the-charts characteristics of this dog.

From the beginning, John and I understood this breed of dog. We also agreed that he was more than likely acquired as a puppy. He was cute and manageable. As the months passed, his natural instincts kicked in, those of a cattle dog, and his previous owners did not understand; apparently not wanting to understand and work with him, they discarded him.

John and I are overjoyed that Doc's previous owners chose our farm to abandon him.

The title, "Doc, a Messenger" was inspired when I witnessed the coming- out of our Josie, when she and Doc bonded. For you see, our Josie, though less frequently, continues to experience flashbacks and night terrors from her puppyhood, when she was hurt, and also, abandoned.

Another word for "messenger" is the word "angel." The light that guided Josie on her incredible journey to us, guided our Doc to her. I knew it, for I saw that light in Doc's eyes when he looked into my eyes.

For anyone who is considering purchasing any breed of canine, I would ask you to remember Josie and Doc's stories when you are actively looking for that special dog. Rescue shelters should be the first place you look, for speaking from experience, these facilities shelter and provide needs for the many abused and abandoned dogs and cats. The people who support these animals are dedicated to helping the many unwanted by sheltering, providing medical needs, food, fostering, and transporting.

Last, but most importantly, when you decide to adopt or purchase a dog, do research on that particular breed, to insure that the dog will fit in with your lifestyle and that you are committed to devoting your time and means to insure that your dog is suited to your environment, and has a good home and family for its lifetime. Dogs deserve nothing less.

Doc is a cattle-herding dog, though we no longer have cattle, our farm setting is ideal for both him and the Labs.

If you have read my first book about the abandonment of Josie, you will understand these precious souls, created by THE ALMIGHTY, will give back to you far more than you give them.

There is a saying, and I quote, "Don't shop. Adopt."

For follow-up, I invite readers to visit my website:

jgeastwoodauthor.com

"The LORD bless you and keep you;
The LORD make His face shine upon you and
be gracious to you; The LORD lift up His countenance
upon you and give you peace."

Numbers 6:24-26 New King James Version

www.ingramcontent.com/pod-product-compliance
Lightning Source LLC
Chambersburg PA
CBHW040155110726
48005CB00018B/2767